LEFT HANDED
HUMMINGBIRD

LEFT HANDED HUMMINGBIRD

JEANINE STEVENS

Clare Songbirds
Publishing House

Clare Songbirds Publishing House Poetry Series
ISBN 978-1-957221-20-5
Clare Songbirds Publishing House
Left Handed Hummingbird© 2025 Jeanine Stevens

Printed in the United States of America
FIRST EDITION

140 Cottage Street
Auburn, New York 13021
www.claresongbirdspub.com

The author wishes to thank the following publications in which these poems first appeared.

Adanna: "Yesterday's Laundry."
Centrifugal Eye: "Left Handed Humming Bird," "In my Dream a Little Boat."
Convergence: "Where Beelines End," "Black Ice."
Cooweescoowee: "Prufrock Eats a Donut."
Edge: "Edging Exotic into Consciousness."
Ekphrasis: "Frida in a White Dress," "*Gelée blanche*," "Composition IX,"
    "Her Name is Yolen."
Eskimo Pie: "Ley Lines."
Evansville Review: "Glass."
Evening Street Review: "Piñon," "Sanctuary."
Exit 13: "Bloodstone."
Forge: "Within a Frame," "Rocket Man," "Winter Coat Tinged Platinum,"
    "Tiny Sun Large Flower."
Illumen: "Compline."
IMPROV: "At the Magpie Café."
Innisfree Poetry Journal: "One Room School House in Fond du lac."
Lummox Press: "Evening News Ghazal."
Late Peaches, Sacramento Anthology 2012: "American Bittern."
Medusa's Kitchen: "People in the Sun," "Scenes from a Marriage Redux,"
    "Poet on a Mountain Top."
Muse: "Bow and Arrow," "Living History."
Nostalgia Magazine: "A New Sun."
POEM: "Autumn Nocturne."
Poet's Espresso: "Derma."
Prenumbra: "Reading a Used Book in July."
Provincetown Magazine: "In this Room Everyone Behaved."
Rattlesnake Press: "A Flat in the City."
Ruah: "little flower."
So It Goes, Journal of the Kurt Vonnegut Memorial Library:
    "Ruins are Never Empty," "The Crying Room."
Tahoe Blues Anthology: "A Narrow Margin of Color."
The MacGuffin: "Watching Hummingbirds with Sun Tzu."
The Poet's Art: "Glimpse."
The Raven's Perch: "Patterns," "Watching Autumn with Tu Fu," "Wild Doll."
Tipton Poetry Journal: "Extinguished Stars," "Tabu," "The Order of Things."
Visions 2024: "Theories at Pech Merle Cave."
Voices 2018: "Tony's on the Pier."
Voices 2023: "At the Community Gardens," "Film Noir."
Winter Rising: "Forecast: November."
Yoga Stanza: "Evensong."

"Bow and Arrow," won the Holden Vaughn Spangler Award, 2022

"Frida in a White Dress," won the Ekphrasis Prize, 2009.
"Her Name is Yolen," received a Pushcart Nomination, 2018.
"In this Room, Everyone Behaved," won the WOMR Cape Cod
    Community Radio National Award, 2016.

Many thanks to those who commented on early drafts of some poems:
Dorianne Laux, David Rigsby, Kim Addonizio, Jimmy Santiago Baca,
Rebecca Morrison, Alexa Mergen, Matthew Zapruder, Forrest Gander,
Diane Frank, Linda Pickens-Jones, Bay Area Poet's Coalition Members
and Kim Wyatt. As always, much appreciation to Tom Goff, editing
and Greg Chalpin, formatting.

CONTENTS

To Gregory and my family

The biggest part of any story is rooms and the things inside them,
an itinerary of small points at two ends of memory.

Donald Revell

I.

GLIMPSE

Bow and Arrow

At the five and dime, hot nuts rotating,
cashews the most expensive,
Spanish peanuts, 10 cents.
Also, arranged in front: greeting cards,
ribbon and thread, packets of sewing needles,
then domestics: bristle brushes,
scouring pads, dish cloths.
Toward the back, the women's section:
pink items disguised in small boxes,
red water bottles and other rubbery things.
A small shelf for men; we didn't go there.
Off to the side, canaries chittering, 75 cents.
Girl's toy section: kits for doll dresses
and jewelry made of dyed macaroni
(we ate before the necklace was finished).
For boys, cap guns, safari hats, sling shots.
My friend and I saved a quarter,
bought a bow and arrow with bright feathers
stapled to cardboard. We never shot the arrows
but walked up and down Kenneth Avenue
just to show what girls could do,
just how useless this could be.
Vonnegut's Hardware was always
good to us, sold a yard of golden bathtub chain
we tucked in one pocket like Zoot Suiters,
and in the other, hot roasted peanuts.

A Flat in the City

Early one Saturday: a knock
at the back door—
"Eli killed Ida." We ran to the corner,
stood across the street
looked up at that window.

It was an ordinary flat. A brown shade
hung listless against the sill.
Shiny flypaper twisted
from the ceiling; you could hear
the black metal fan's constant whip and drone.

They mostly sat in the kitchen,
he in his undershirt reading the news,
smoking, drinking coffee,
she, in a zippered house dress,
brown and white checks spattered
with little daisies,
the kind you order from a catalogue.

Once, she gave us lemonade.
When she opened a window, he would yell,
"Shut that, flies are coming in!"

Was it the corncakes fried in three inches
of lard, the mid-West heat,
dust balls in the corner?

Or something else I was too young
to know: flawed zipper, worn
electrical cord, or empty toothpaste can?

Perhaps that speckled spot on her neck,
growing, the suffering to come,
and not being able to live without her.

Glimpse

A young woman's hands cradle
a dying man. I wonder

    what hands have come before:

hands that swaddled him as an infant
(in what we called receiving blankets)

    hands that washed tiny paws
filled with mud cakes at play

    rubbed tired shoulders ill
with childhood maladies

    hands that shook his on graduation,
new job, new marriage

his own hands brushing a daughter's hair
or helping her lace her ice skates

hands that held fresh wood
for his wife's own private workroom

    hands that reached inside
for warmth and flowers.

Living History

Someone rearranged all the rooms:
bed and dresser in the dining area,
    family photos lopsided
in the kitchen sink, crock pots

    askew on bookshelves,
    all my volumes in the Jacuzzi.

Where the computer stood,
the weed eater has a place of honor.
Holiday decorations droop
from the ceiling fan. My pink leotard
    hides the Tiffany lamp.

Our Havilland (Troy pattern) serves
as everyday dishes;
nuts and bolts fill the utensil drawer,
the motorcycle in disrepair
greasy on the Berber carpet.

No more lobster and quinoa,
now the freezer full of fries and cheap cuts.
Worst of all, the piano tilts on an outside wall
moistened by green spores.

How could a docent explain?
A topsy-turvy dream, remnants
of an estate sale, or is this how you'll live
    when I'm gone?

Ruins Are Never Empty

First freedom, beginner's rollers, felt laces
over the toe, then clamp-ons
with ball bearings, faster over cracked sidewalks.
Steel key (Chicago Skate Co.)
on a grocer's string around our necks.
    We owned these streets.

Then, bikes, maroon and blue, we flew past
grandfather's house, pedaling
through university grounds.
Out on Meridian Street to fancier homes,
up the drive, a maid flapping a kitchen towel,
    shooing us like barnyard chickens.

Further out, our favorite, an abandoned estate,
matching urns with bird's nests
and cigarette butts. Crushed glass everywhere
crackling gold in the sun.

We sat on steps, imagined souls who lived here:
magnificent banquets, green holly and red ribbons,
hired musicians and barcarolles,
uncles with sweet pipes, scent
of lavender in the linens.

And in summer, striped canopies,
boys with short trousers,
shrimp on toast points, imprints
everywhere. Straying too far,
    tires flat, a long walk home.

Yesterday's Laundry

Light is the moon and my mother's name. Wait
for the angle and curve. Next thought is Sunday

after a slow week, a cavalcade of false urgencies,
fake news. Take a slow drive along the turnpike,

traffic signs spilling green neon. Miles of going.
Did I unplug my iron; put the roast in the oven?

An ad for Big O Tires reminds me of the seatbelt
recall. Why am I driving among RAV4'S

and Hondas when meditating with my olivella
shell seems more reasonable? Bee Hive Cluster

flashes like a monk's retreat on remote islands,
What shines through grabs me. Midnight.

Nothing burning. Mother asks, "Why
is yesterday's wash still pinned to the line?"

At the Community Garden
Locke, California

Autumn, dry husks rattle.
Overhead, a raven creases the sun.
Poets compete with crickets,
someone BBQs, salads and wine served.
Under the green apple and gnarled cherry,
red poppies spin
toward the mic to hear good words.

In the garden, new cabbages and corn,
wrinkled chard from last season grows five feet high.
In old times: bitter melon, long bean and luffa.
Among furrowed rows, I'm certain the purple chicken
standing on one leg has something to tell.

A Chinese town, where settlers came across the water.
Some say at night you can still see the flash
of yellow lanterns in and out of grassy banks,
riparian zone, tangle of vines and shrubs.

Early fog burns on storefronts
and breezes blow webs across old glass.
In dim light, a room may appear, crimson wallpaper
with phoenix, side chair with green dragon.

Perhaps fragments: brass bells and wind chimes.
Is that the scent of clove from porcelain cups?
A heavy sigh that is not the wind.

Do meandering souls still come from the river,
fluff a porch pillow or wait by the window?
Do they wonder over our strange foods:
potato salad and cheesecake?

A woman sits beside me. "I want to show you."
She unsnaps her silk purse, takes out
a jade amulet, gold earrings.
"From my family, the old country,
to sell if my husband in this new place is mean to me."

The hem of her shimmery dress frays.
I dare not pull a loose thread—
the entire scene may disappear.

Love Lies Bleeding

The colorful packet promised rhubarb-red fleshy stalks,
pendulous blossoms, love tails, drooping rags of chenille.

For some, this spectacular bloom meant hopeless love,
reminded Bernie Taupin what touring did to family life.

Aztecs popped the seeds like corn, seeds for pain,
or mashed with human blood to sculpt bodies of Gods.

By fall, a dull old gold, color of illness, a drooping
underworld. Couldn't wait to clear the waste.

Midwinter walk, flower beds raked clean,
except for the neighbor's stalks, half their size,

bent toward the road, shrunken like old men,
sharp acorn chips caught in ragged beards,

In recovery, he leaves bent tassels until spring,
bearing witness to fallow fields, the lessons of autumn.

The Order of Things

Wanting a quick break from revisions,
I order the tomato bisque and coffee
at La Bou, settle in for a long lunch.

From the bus stop on Watt Avenue,
a stately woman comes in with large backpack
and rolling duffel that was once expensive.
Stylish in cherry red sweater,
black pants and worn clogs, she orders
a small coffee and sits close to me.

She takes bottles of water and large paper
cups from her backpack, pours
something into one cup
which goes directly into the microwave.

She sniffs, eats the contents.
I'm not sure if it's bread or meat?
In the other cup, fresh water also
microwaved, cooled, another bottle filled.

She leaves the coffee untouched, purchased
so she can come in and prepare her lunch.

Bred to Shine

Stars, solar dust, strata.
 The first magnificent fracture, cell division,
  magic of sperm and ovum,
   most tumbling, missing a turn.

We are a random breed,
 so few chosen,
  the absent sisters,
   the ones with gifts of song.

I think of old woodcuts, midnight,
 ladies and gents marveling at the arc,
  stars embedded in mesh reflecting on the Rhine,
   shimmer, float
    on small eddies, a gentle tide.

Creamy watercolors, abstract orbs and points,
 more like liquefied daffodils cartwheeling
  across the Galaxy, a swirl swathed in buttermilk.

Do you notice by midafternoon how boldest flowers stretch
 necks, follow the sun from the Sierras—
  to the Pacific?

In a rock face, new fissures appear,
 small weeds emerge;
  hairline cracks—
   flaws we all love.

Deserted Holiday

We come to deal with grief and avoid solitude:
walk Union Square, visit grand hotels
with ornate staircases.

Watching the lighting of the tree
from the Starlight Lounge twenty one floors up,
we pay a fortune for high-end drinks.

We do not have roast turkey with oyster stuffing,
no pecan pie, no freshly ironed linen cloth,
no centerpiece of winter squash.

Instead, Pacific salmon, wild rice and tiramisu
at a small table with other tourists, some
complaining the salmon is undercooked.

Next day, past bustling Chinatown
we visit North Beach, tables set al fresco:
Today's Special: Rigatoni and Chianti.

We backtrack to City Lights Books,
relax in overstuffed chairs in the poetry section.
I purchase *Saving Twilight,* Julio Cortázar,
caught by his photo sitting on the floor,
smiling, so happy talking to his cat.

Heading home, on our left, Alcatraz,
the lone stone edifice
— Corso's deserted holiday.

We enter the family room,
an unopened box of decorations wait:
angels and snowflakes, made by tiny hands.

Tabu

Late summer. I uproot
tomato and radish,
turn over for spring fodder,
        more than pungent, over-ripe, cruciferous.

Reminiscent
of my parent's vast double bed,
        their room warmer, the sheets softer.

Heavy odor I still can't identify.
Sex, sweat,
        remnants of whiskey sours
        and buttered scallops,
                somehow a comfort.

And always perfume's faint mystery:

Tabu, its violin shaped bottle
        and *20 Carats*, gold flecks resting
                on the bottom.

It seemed I was always on the edge
of what was forbidden.

Now, looking again
the ground up vegetables in uneven rows
        seem like brightest
                cloaks of red-lipped tulips.

Scenes from a Marriage Redux

1973. In that decade, everything was Swedish,
songs of a summer night, wild strawberries,
and Marianne and Johan in the six-part
disintegration of a marriage.

I gave my class in "Family Studies"
the option of attending the film
or writing a term paper on communication.
I was surprised so many came,
but after all, the J Street Theater was the first
to serve coffee, espresso in little cups.

Agonizing sequences of Sunday dinners
at Marianne's parents resulted in day long
squabbles and blame.
Marianne and Johan, by their own admission,
were incapable of marriage,
yet too insecure to leave.
"Emotional illiterates," he said.

2003. I hadn't thought much about Bergman
until a film in this new century,
Sarabande, featuring Marianne and Johan
together as friends.
He comes to her bed with wet PJs.
Memories, hopes and fantasies,
or is this another kind of caring
I have yet to learn.

Film Noir

Men will be clean shaven and wear hats in a Film Noir,
add in shiny shoes and pinstripe suits in a Film Noir.

Get a whiff of cigar smoke, wet stub, ashes the color
of bone, a gruff voice, and heavy jowls in a Film Noir.

You will rarely see a woman in a flowered dress
but a thin gun moll in slinky satin in a Film Noir.

Dark scenes except for one dull bulb in an all-night café.
Hear the globes snap off the theater marquee in a Film Noir?

No croissants or French press in a fancy bistro, but wedge
of homemade pie and thick mug of Joe in a Film Noir.

No angel with golden halo and tissue thin wings, just
a cracked cherub on top the deserted church in a Film Noir.

You will see a piece of paper blowing around a lamppost:
perhaps a movie script or faded celluloid in a Film Noir?

No blood red dahlia, but catch Nat King Cole's lilting
version of "Blue Gardenia," at the Tiki Room in a Film Noir.

The Crying Room

Located in a dark corner of the Ritz Theater,
it was a small room with loge seating,
a glassed-in wall for viewing.

A speaker system piped in tinny dialogue.
I assumed the room was for women
overcome with emotion
who might disturb other patrons.

My mother always talked about
"Now Voyager," with Bette Davis,
how she couldn't contain the tears.

I wanted mother all to myself,
waited on the back steps.
She opened the screen door,
large pocketbook in hand, baby
sister on her hip,

      "I'm coming with you."

I became nauseous from the smell
of Chesterfields and baby spit.
One started crying, then all wailed in unison.
The mothers didn't seem to mind.

I moved outside
to a single seat on the aisle.

II.

EDGING EXOTIC

Extinguished Stars

There is no end to the simplest journey,
especially at 2 A.M. Refreshed,
four hours sleep and ready for a new route.
I ruminate, what in the 60's
we called "monkey mind,"
up to its nightly games, zipping convolutions,
seeking useless scraps of information.
Did I lock the door?
Arranged for automatic deposit?
Every time I try to narrow my intent,
more scenarios appear. I focus
on the alleyway I walked as a child,
my version of counting sheep.
Fuchsia hollyhocks beamed along back fences,
trash cans sprayed with DDT stood open.
Faces of my teachers: stern Mrs. Overheiser,
Mrs. Stack and Mrs. Lloyd,
the ones I learned the most from.
I see the backyard where boys played pirate,
tied others to posts and lit them on fire.
Now, 4 A.M., keeping time,
I try my mantras: Peace, Om.
At the edge where the alleyway meets 37th St,
I hesitate; realize how vast this matter, this chatter.
I'm confounded by my memory stream,
sit down next to a deep crack,
ready to invest in new images.
Dreaded dawn leaks pale and slack
through Venetian blinds.
This is *the hour for those past thirty*
when the wind blows from extinguished stars.
Do you hear what I hear? *A book of verse,*
yeast rising, a new tune? The morning
paper slaps the porch: from my oven,
warm cinnamon rolls with sultanas.

Vapor

When young, a favorite line: "Borne like a vapor
on the summer's air" (Stephen Foster).
When I received the assignment in 10th grade:
"Choose a work of art and live with it all semester,"
I immediately selected Botticelli's *Birth of Venus*.
Air balmy and blue—she stood
on a creamy white scallop shell.
No floundering, no tottering but upright,
born in the sea, a body I thought ideal,
although mine wasn't quite there yet.
Zephyr, god of the west wind, and Aura,
god of breath, gently blew her toward shore,
a lush garden of deep laurel, the entire piece
so flowery, posies everywhere. Hora, goddess
of the seasons, waited with dress and robe,
fabric airy as a hankie, what we called lawn,
the design so kept and precise. Years later,
in Florence, on a steamy July, looking
at the original, the painting faded.
Venus hasn't touched land yet,
Hora still waiting. But, the waves gentle,
salt spray refreshing, hint of frangipani and pine.

Venus on the Half Shell
Collage by Alice Czalpinski

Modeled after Botticelli, yet no lush trees
or rosebuds. Stark pink palms, rough land—
you can almost touch the grit.

No creamy scallop shell, she balances
on a spiny sea urchin and yellowing clam.

No breathy gods as guide.
Coral fans and brown kelp nudge her
to a rocky shore.

Not the voluptuous Venus of prehistory,
excavated over a wide geography,
this one slender.

Slim legs carved to a point, perfect for poking
into the ground near the evening fire,

purple shadow magnified, writhing:
totem, fetish, goddess? The only facial features,

stark eyes, a look of surprise. She floats
in front of an ancient map of the Black Sea.

Pecked motifs in her hair, shoulders and hips,
Moldovan folk designs near the Ukrainian border.

Theories at Pech Merle Cave
~with Bob Creeley, 2004

What does it mean, this cave, this century?
At five, I hid in the closet with a pink girdle
and broken violin, yet felt safe.
Here, it is cold, dripping, damp.

Dotted horses, shaggy mammoths—
I hear heavy breathing,
their lope and gallop pounding across a landscape,
bruised odor of trampled grass.
How intriguing, painted men,
black spears protruding from stick bodies.
Imaginary wounds from trance?

Our guide switches off her flashlight:
shadow's dusky scents,
not mildew, not unpleasant.
We wonder how to enter the time gap
between recorded history and 25,000 years ago.

Bob clears his throat, "Belief in heaven, perhaps
an attempt to leave the cave?"
I think of Queen of the Night set design,
star charts, pinpoint lights poking blue velvet,
yet on this ceiling, no comet, nebula, black hole.

Bob continues, "How about the head as cathedral?
I suggest brain as labyrinth, convolutions,
blood memories floating, frescos
etched before birth on walls of our skulls.
Perhaps pictures as first scripture?

In the evening, nothing settled, a pot of tea;
we talk of daily pleasures at home,
NPR and the rose garden.

Soon summer ends, we return to the classroom,
try to answer the simpler questions.

Within a Frame
Photo of Jean Cocteau by Man Ray 1922

A young Jean peers through an empty frame.
Skin shines over thin knuckles.

Smart suit of clothes expertly tailored,
collar starched polar white, so bright it must be new.

Hair fluffed high with pomade, I detect
expensive cologne,
yet a solemn expression
perhaps to discount his idle nickname:
"The frivolous prince."

On his left wrist, a twisted string,
one of those devices to remember which day it is,
which appointment to keep, when
other Bohemians, his coterie of friends,
will meet at his favorite bar,
    Le Boeuf sur le Toit.

In the blurred background, bust on a pedestal,
nondescript, an unknown face—
a prop?
Is everything in art intentional?

Perhaps shadow to his persona; hidden brilliance.
He will create a "beast house"
where door knockers grimace and latches grin

as in *La Belle et la Bête* around 1979.
Is this the same young man who designed
screaming keyholes, animated portraits?

Rocket Man

Sitting by the window, I fluff the tapestry pillow,
yellow with red chickens on gold muslin.

Outside, variegated ivy in shade,
drenching rain, ground still spongy.

On TV, one more politician resigned, fired?
Still draining the swamp that extended from

northern Indiana to D.C. I read a line of poetry:
"For a long time my brother wore Rocket Man

pajamas & Nothing: The body
never lies."

What more can we expect?
What more of strategies?

An ordinary barnyard, chicks scrambling,
hen cowering, pecking order obvious.

Black Ice

Shops that cater to vacationers closed.
If you want a post card or souvenir shot glass,
check out the local CVS.
The slow cadence of late Autumn, a good time
to check the spatter of moth holes
on wool cardigans.
Ice and snow set limits on choices.

A local bookseller remains open.
Hardy poets stage a costume party:
one dressed as Sexton curses a dog,
another as Hefner in a silk dressing gown
looks amused. Someone brings absinthe.
Black ice appears on the road.

A pause before the Italians arrive,
blond women and gorgeous men,
designer ski togs and gold jewelry,
antsy to hit the slopes.
Locals pack a lunch, retreat to the lake
and count the bald eagles nesting.

Winter Coat Tinged Platinum
South Lake Tahoe

I'm returning home, early spring.
100 yards ahead, a coyote crosses the road,
fluffy white, yellow, gray like a big blond fox.
I stop, raise my arm in salute
not sure if this is a right gesture.

       Watching, turning
            toward me, a long time.

Something familiar, head and shoulders foreshortened
like the giraffe pictograph, the Fezzan,
North Africa, 100 B.C.
       Same stance, hesitation,
no threat, something beyond curiosity?

He trots on, probably to trash bins
behind Safeway,
winter coat tinged platinum;
curved back mimics
Mount Rose in the distance.

Later, sitting by the woodstove snapping cedar,
what to make of contact with topaz eyes,
       wild fur, the edge of things?
I think artifact—
look at my Washoe basket, buck saw,
map of prehistoric game trails.

The cabin warms; ice chunks slide
from the tin roof.
On the Tamarack, a Red-headed woodpecker
chisels out another unwritten code.

Forecast: November

Summer residents have left the mountain,
windows boarded up, a scatter of folks
who stay through the winter.
As I walk, sky darkens, time to turn back,
but just ahead a flickering orange.
I wonder: dancing elves, a gnome's abode?
Closer, the site looks festive.
Twinkle lights strung over
the make-shift bar, TV hanging under the eaves
(Notre Dame and Northwestern tied).
Chairs set up around a sparking fire,
safely contained in iron mesh.
I'm invited to sit with three men, one
gets married tomorrow. He shakes my hand,
rough, a worker's hand. They drink
something brown over ice.
"Women are inside cooking," they say.
Visiting from the Delta, "river rats"
they call themselves. I want to ask
their opinion on proposed tunnels to divert water.
One wears a cap with ear flaps,
a bachelor party, not the time for politics.
I consider walking home
to get the ½ bottle of Korbel.
The groom says his name is Cal.
A lot of men in his generation
are named Cal. He calls me Blondie,
offers his pipe, dark red, carved design
something like a dragon.
I say no and thanks, not my party.
He waits until I leave to lite up.

Komodo
"Enlightenment," Painting by Katie Ruiz

Like a Mesoamerican pyramid,
massive architecture, vast and wide,
stripes of tangerine, canary, scarlet Macaw,

creeping things: turtles, monkeys, jaguars,
form reminiscent of the seven story mountain
where one finds wisdom by traveling through layers,

noticing plants and animals: tigers in the orange garden,
lizards in the green. First you must maneuver a vast
jungle of exotic growth: papyrus, mandrake, bromeliad.

Take a whiff of patchouli sweet and savage. At first glance,
foliage seems playful, but look again—Komodo dragon under
a fluffy forest in Borneo. Are those feathers, leaves, a poisonous

breed of centipede, a newborn in that pea pod? At a distance, another
mirage for enlightenment or the artists dream of a simpler mole hill?
Before the first step, let's raise a silver cup overflowing with dark rum.

Left Handed Hummingbird

It had something to do with ashes and canoes
in an old file. I research:

The Left Handed Hummingbird,
"Bird from the south, God of War and Sun."

Green appears: the tongue, a split reed, thrums
soggy banks, searching for gazania
or any flower with a black dotted center.

I have seen it, this immigrant escaping
the parched zone, feeding
on white verbascum in a deserted village.

I can imagine in some other world,
hummingbirds racing through Aztec ball courts,
grand avenues, flashing red ahead of creation.

Unsure of origins, powers and gifts,
anointed quills write with crushed oak galls
mixed with gold nectar, the formula for ink.

Sounding familiar, I research: *The Weeping Eye.*

The arched brow, once cosmetic,
then cast as sacred, slips into water, seeks
the Mexican coast, the gulf, the big river north.

Pyramids stride the Mississippi:
gorget, shell and column, tears hidden
under a canopy of eagle's feathers.

Monk's Mound, Cahokia, Illinois, (900-955 CE),
population,10-20,000, much larger than Paris
at the time. Diet of corn, beans, and squash
surpassed that of wealthy Europeans.

The left wing opens, green ink brilliant in thin veins,
scores maps of watersheds, etches the lost eye above
my wrist, then drops its darker seed into my palm.

Edging Exotic into Consciousness

White space as breath holds narrow interstice, a small pocket
that grows multitudinous inhaling the entire Arctic Sea.
   The scent of balsam

as from stately firs is gobbled up as fragrance by hungry
lungs. Incense becomes smoke, slips down vessel and tissue
   to mid-section. Even if

tarnished like an acid etched mirror, belly wants its share,
devours all, nothing frittered away. Rumblings of metaphor,
   the is-ness

of mulled-over images chewed into morsels, reformed,
released to rest in golden channels. The conduit is assembled,
   the smoke extinguished.

If my thigh feels chafed and I rubbed hard enough,
what would emerge? This great human shank sprung from
   the center of green?

Ley Lines

How melodious the sound,
pilgrimage guideposts, ancient trackways
aligned along ridge tops,
stone protrusions and hillforts like sentinels,
linked by mystical, magnetic forces.

Follow a fieldstone wall;
walk to a small village!
In clumps of trees,
find old crockery hidden in pine branches.
    Place an amulet there.

Amid banks of glittering chicory and cress,
icy streams cascade over the North Downs.

Walk northwest. Take a boat to Iona,
Iona in its solitude, old light and stone crosses.
Notice the soft colors of worn books
in the simply hewn library.

Make your own line-of-sight navigation,
your own map of the world
as when Krishna's mother opened
    his mouth full of sand
and discovered the sparkling universe inside.

Why do we admire the ancients so,
their begging bowls, their broth?

When you come to an end,
graph your journey, begin again.
Ask a red hawk to come with you.

Evening News Ghazal

International Space Station Flies Over at 6:40 P.M, noted
on the evening news. My naked eye captures this white
    star, soft-caught on the evening news.

Picasso's bright clouds, as blurbs hastily written, puff and
hoot the moon. A tired trombone player toots the jazziest
    of tunes, while watching the evening news.

An anxious hunch, the ebony bull waits his turn to bellow.
Last year in Nigeria, 100,000 elephants poached, this just
    received in a dispatch by the evening news.

In the fun house, white chunks like teeth in the mouth
of a carnival ride, swallow me whole as I make a last tour
    in my little green car, stalked by the evening news.

Another Roadside Bomb in Kabul, 86 Dead (or is it 87?).
In artificial light, camera zooms to a boy in homespun robe,
    muddied face, his story botched on the evening news.

Eyes rimmed red, slow moving tears stain the smudged
cheek, a composite of persons missing every day, just in
    time to be taught on the evening news.

Is it distance that makes such glimmering? Technology
reveals crossings so clearly, dark and light, both costly,
    warp and weft faintly stitched on the evening news.

A special about past decades—Nixon paired with a long-
distance runner. Photo and story grossly mismatched
    by the evening news.

Clicking maracas X-out the wind; Pablo's fleshy
dancers, like penny kangaroos spell out a milky MOO.
    This story hastily hacked by the evening news.

III.

EVENSONG

Composition IX

Off-color rainbow,
magenta, spruce and slate,
caps the inked heart,
        a heart in motion.

Black stick eyes,
or are they stitched—deft lashes
blink right, blink left:
        a warrior's headdress.

Limpet's foot
drags a kite tail through amber canyons.

Art that is a mountain,
low burning creosote, mute scarlet
        splitting stones.

A slight smear, background sun
sweeps star shadows:
        a tale to tell.

In the shade, a painted desert,
something of Arizona: Navaho.

The heart that is
        a heart that holds.

At the Magpie Café
~with Joan

I arrive early and sit at a plain wood table,
notice small water glasses where patrons
help themselves
not like the plastic tankards at Red Lobster.

Brown recycled napkins are available
not the flurry of cloth at the Hilton.

The cardboard menus are printed
on the backs of yesterday's fare.
My tea is presented in a white cup
with saucer rather than a giant mug.

Under the cup, a square doily cut
from worn luncheon menus featuring:
Winter Squash Panini, Salad Trio
and Vietnamese Tri Tip.

Bloodstone

In this latest Sierra blaze, early skies
sear with smoke, everything
cast exotic:
granite path bronzed,
wood gazebo backlit by pewter glint.
The fragrant *Osmanthus*, usually exuding
heady perfume…holds her breath.

Our bodies flare;
we dream in striped tents,
rough elbows smoothed
    to a burnished copper,
corridors of dawn counted in amber veils.

Is it true, too much fire may consume,
choke oxygen, reduce passion to purpling ash?

The oil painting by your father:
charred palms, red sky and gold tipped clouds—

    a typical Pacific sunset

    cautionary shadows

    or ancient grove inflamed?

A hummer hovers between heartbeats,
confused by the metal wind chime,
its pearl moon now bloodstone.

Only the lustrous black bee retains true color
sucking oblivious in the morning glory pool.

Extravagance
Mary of Bethany, after John 12: 1-8

They say I was extravagant, pricey oil in that alabaster jug,
my only inheritance, my only bride price.
He sat telling stories of treasures, moths and vermin,
not heard anywhere else on earth.

I was overjoyed, sweaty palms, something
beyond devotion, felt like a seer
with special powers as I untied the leather thong
from my hair, let it cascade over the dusty,
delicate feet, masculine and strong.
Oil on my fingers, first the arch,
then toes, taut tendons,
trying to rub away treachery.

My hair swirled, bathed in dripping essential oil,
Spikenard, virgin, with essence of olive, herbs,
some say honeysuckle. My best homespun dress
stained and fragrant, most of the jug emptied.

Martha clanked plates and spoons in the kitchen.
We've talked about this before, her cooking, me idling.
She said, "The oldest has other advantages, so go ahead,
who knows what harkening angel is around the corner."

Looking back, was this a mistake, squandering
my choices? There were options: stay home,
tend the fire, care for the elderly. Or marry
the brick mason—my past wasn't important to him.

I can still smell the odor of mutton fat,
the house filled with perfume. Even now,
the hem of that dress— still pliable with oil.

Dance of Miriam
~Marc Chagall

"Dance me through the panic
till I'm gathered safely in."
Leonard Cohen

On dry land, she grabs her timbrel,
bare feet kick up ancient dust,
Yemenite steps trace designs in the earth.

Rounded breasts like honeydews,
bright blue wrap-a-round
her only clothing.
Bracelets and bangles sparkling,
her skin flushed with salt.

Women join in, more drums, songs, bells
flashing in the sun.
Startled, larks fly in to see.

Twin goats arrive with their sweet milk.
Air is drenched in tangerine and lime.
A flowering shrub so red it blisters,
shoots fireworks of white stars.

Looking back, horse and rider
still tumbling into the boiling sea.
Miriam keeps dancing, dancing
until all have traveled on.

Derma

Skin…first universe greets dawn, tough hide
we live in, bargain with.
Skin as landscape: mountain spasm—
shoulders as hillock, tears waterfall, hair
tangled thicket, dry heel
cracked Mojave,
long shank—Coast Redwood.

Aerial photographs reveal hidden cities,
kettle ponds or lake.
What is our exterior plot plan?
Too much smut watching,
novel reading discoloring pigment?
Goose bumps fear the clutching spine,
the scalp, the crown.

Oh, for a full night's sleep,
no twitching, eye clear to distinguish the freckle
from the mole, crow from the raven.

Warm stones on the lower back always a good idea.
Marrow bone soup for aging,
a balm to soften the craggy jaw.

Illustrated man.
Skin as threshold.

Frida in a White Dress

More beautiful than self portraits
with monkeys and snakes,
in pristine lace, like a
communion dress, you are all
purity and grace.
The cigarette, casually
caught in your left hand,
the tip rosy, glowing,
seems to mock the girlish
eyelet, the puffy sleeves.
Overlarge beads mask
the gorget at your throat,
reminiscent of the spiraling sun,
iridescent, like the patch of armor
on the neck of a hummingbird.
You flick grey ash
into the three-legged bowl,
a replica of ancient sacrificial
lamps, the kind now used for salsa.
Dark palms blur
against the stucco wall—
as they must
from cradling so much light.

Against Insomnia

The open gate in obscure shadow
tuberose eaten by goats
mirrors in uneven corridors
automatic voices from an eternal zone.
I have familiar questions
but appreciate the obvious.

Now a slow tambourine etched with poems,
a troubadour beating old rhythms.
Rumors silent, objects decompose,
the party breaks up and people search for aviaries.
The resident cobra rests,
cares not for the public show, the illegal mirror.

Hasty voices from the cantina,
call for more chick peas, more humus;
instead a constant supply of frijoles served.
Anytime now, a crucial bulletin—
"Who tore the photo of hacienda and tree?"
Unobscured by dusk,
the vain entertainers go on.

Evensong

Near the levee west of Lodi
I wait for this holy herd.
God has pledged beauty.
I haven't asked, but have hope
this Sunday.

Out day-feeding,
Sandhill Cranes in the distance,
resemble flocks of grazing sheep.

Suddenly airborne,
sounding like a thousand loping horses
long gray necks haul bustles awash
in bright ochre, gallop
along the flyway, a private corridor
invisible to my naked eye.

You don't have to sit in cathedrals,
listen to sermons, place
offerings in the till.
Simply wait, look

for vast, watery beds,
a feathered sanctuary expecting
the moon to open

her pewter eye, scan still
silhouettes and call them her own.

Sanctuary

Sitting on my deck, sprig of sweet woodruff
floating in May wine.

Glancing at the linden, her umbrella branches
a dense canopy. Low sun
illuminates the small Buddha, once bright verdigris,
now peeling from frost and rain.

Patches of pale yellow light shimmer
on his young face,
blotchy surface like a relic
from a long forgotten Cambodian temple
set in this miniature jungle
of dark-stemmed mint, wild garlic and variegated ivy.

Even though mottled, he remains slim,
serene with plaited hair, no pot belly,
much as he first appeared
on a tidal wave with no wind.
I recognize my own fine lines, deepening crevices,
wiry hair, thinner bones.

Light edges toward solstice and summer thunder.
Against the fence, a terra cotta St. Francis holds
a dove's nest, flimsy and dear.
A peaceful sanctuary growing here unnoticed:
one tree, one god, one saint.

43

Where Beelines End
~a Cento

I saw once, in what had been the pleasure-garden
of the popes at Avignon,

blond bell-pulls of bloom. The mid-air
resort of honeybees' hirsute cotillion.

Let gardens grow where beelines end,
sighing in roses, saffron blooms, buddleia;
where bees pray on their knees.

Some, even now, are dying at the end
of their few weeks, some being born in the dark.

Bees have gathered somewhere like petals
closing for the coming of the cold.

The silhouette of a sphinx moth swerves
to drink at the flowerhead.

Gelée blanche
Hoarfrost, Camille Pissarro

With stout walking staff, the farmer trudges
uphill, bent with his bundle
of kindling for the evening fire.
Shadows bend with the terrain,
defoliated in winter haze.
Opaque glare glazes
over purple ribbed furrows.
How intriguing to add swatches
of slick hoarfrost, like a patchwork
clipped and laid in place
on carefully tilled earth,
what Pissarro called his *Snow Effect*.
At the bottom of the swale,
imagine the artist just out of frame,
warm brazier and small stool
under his grey umbrella. Pungent
waste rags with too much color
scatter and stiffen.
He is excited by the cartilage
of this new work: arc lines, delicate clavicles.
As his outer mood directs bones
of the landscape, the inner explores
the beauty of absence.
I don't agree with the critic that says
an entire grove is missing.
Notice a suggestion of pollarded willows
lining the stream, reaching trunks
made even more wavy
by earth's curvature, the entire piece
a caged windbreak.
Small shrubs dissolve
into flaming garnet clumps.
The walker continues uphill,
soft crush of ice underfoot.
All is metered,
slow stride in tomorrow's sun.

One Room School House in Fond du lac
~ *for my Mother*

Uncle Jon warms bricks for our feet.
The horse snorts white clouds in icy air.
    We cross the river in frozen dark,
pull blankets over our shoulders.

In the schoolroom, I fill a large pan
with water, place it on the iron woodstove
    heat lunches in glass jars—
leftovers: soup, stew, bacon chunks and bread.

Older students work on their own,
today—geography. Chile is a red slash
    on the map (we are told, "Pronounce it She-lay")
a bright spot lighting up homespun and denim.

By afternoon, windows steam.
Younger children practice cursives:
    up, down, down, down—thick pencils
scratch, boots tap and scrape the raspy floor.

Uncle Jon warms bricks for the ride home.
On our laps, quilt squares hold pale sun.
    In the dusk, the river is gray and bleak
and the horse must be fed before dark.

46

Tiny Sun, Large Flower

So we live on a fireball, ride a molten orb,
children of citrus rind, of sunflower.

I read the earth's core, 11,000 degrees F.
same temperature
as the sun's surface.

Then the sun in Arles, otherworldly,
even the vicious mistral
born of two competing winds
cannot interfere
with light making whites alabaster,
blues peacock, yellows mustard.
Not one depressing shade or gloomy hue.

(There is a town that never receives sun.
How can people be normal: no solstice,
    night music, night madness?)

No wonder Vincent dipped his brush so deep,
    internal fire, eternal fire.

Even fish glimmer celadon, escargot shine pearl,
and peonies burn ruby on hillsides.

Tony's on the Pier

Here at Redondo Beach with cousins
in the 1950s, met my first love on the sand,
wild in the scent of burnt skin, salt and sweat.

The splintered observation deck overlooks
a weary Pacific. I talk to others here
on recommendations from Trip Advisor.

Not a casual visit but one to say goodbye,
a last relative from all those
who came west to work in the industry:
Hughes, Douglas, Boeing.

The Foster's Freeze is gone,
and the thrift shop where we bought
out-of-date Navy uniforms,
a white sharkskin blazer with gold buttons
I wore all through high school.

On the bar, a souvenir, larger than a shot glass,
probably an Old Fashioned.
Touristy design— sturdy pilasters
support the deck, inky waves reach underneath,
black palms clump near a vacant shore
and somewhere the soundtrack, *Victory at Sea.*

Compline

Evening comes
with all the finished hours.
In Tai Chi, I find the needle in the sea
where the white snake creeps down.

Evening comes with all
the finished hours. Late coffee at La Bou,
a fifth re-vision of my Milwaukee poem.

Evening comes with
finished hours: the evening meal— salmon,
greens, the Colbert report with logo:
a screeching eagle I learn is actually a hawk.

Evening comes, my book
about a burial finished, an unwed mother faces
West, the fetus faces East.

Evening. Liquid gold
leaks under the redwood trees, twin skunks
dance a midnight nocturne.

Her Name is Yolen

Dressed in grays, browns, monochromatic chalk
except the carmine and emerald scarf

protecting your head, the rust blanket carrying
your wares. Squatting, as if looking for rich tubers

to harvest, but this ground is dirt rough and poor,
Haiti's topsoil eroded to bedrock. Yet, handmade

biscuits gather around you, over 100 palm-size edible
cakes to sell at the market in Port-au-Prince.

What industry in your work! I want to touch, so smooth,
uniform, die-cut precision patterned in sand and gravel.

Treasures to display among other artisans, brilliant
birds and geckos on tin, those who offer Moringa

seedlings in small pots to try the earth again, flout
erosion in a land rebuilding from yet another quake.

Short of breath, my throat dry, I try to imagine
chewing, swallowing these discs made of clay

a traditional supplement for pregnant women—
clay (iron and calcium), salt and shortening added.

And what of clay? We are clay, what good sense—
clay gathered from the river, the right

amount of moisture required to hold ingredients together—
animal, vegetable, mineral.
                              ~Carbon Footprints: Minimal

Reading a Used Book in July

I relax into the lawn chair,
open *Fifty Years of American Poetry*
from the free-bin at the local library.
This little Dell paperback
so old, the spine cracks,
the glue disintegrates,
and pages fall away to poems
that must have been someone's favorites.
I doze, then wake to words:
lustful, fickle, elegiac and spellbinding.

We come to the mountains
for a few quiet days, too early
for the crimson kokanee to spawn.
Perhaps I will write about Canada geese,
lichen, even graffiti. Someone painted
the name Neva on fences and granite outcrops.
We wonder about Neva.

Yesterday, by the front door at the Chinese Buffet,
a gnawed bone lay in the dirt planter
without even the token
plastic flowers. Not good for business.
Here are some lines:
a Swedish pool boy
a patchwork scrap bag
a receipt for nail polish from Monoprix.

The sun slips behind the summit.
I put root vegetables in the steamer, realize
I've left my rock cod too long on the side board.
You fiddle with the new antenna,
try to get the Summer Olympics from Reno.

A page breaks loose, lands on the fish.
Why write unless you praise the sacred places,
a line now wet and glutinous.
Later a cleansing swim in the lake.

A New Sun

There is a story about a fig tree in a vineyard,
no fruit after three years. Depleting the soil?
Cut it down? Give it one more year, dig
and fertilize. I think of the poster from the 1970's,
a spindly daisy, *Bloom Where You Are Planted*.
Perhaps some environments are just wrong,
clogged, spoiled. My new variety of geraniums,
"Presto Pink Sizzle," the soil matted
with black roots like fine wires, dense pad
of steel wool. No blooms and the leaves
turned yellow. Transplanted to a new pot,
sprouting magenta and rose the next day.
As with people, not every street, every
horizon is the best. Growing up
in the mid-west with freezing winters,
black soot from the basement furnace,
I watched my brother languish. Small
in stature, ear trouble, bullied and teased.
I stepped between fights, got in a couple of blows.
Dad hooked a punching bag in the basement
to toughen him up. In tears, at summer camp,
we picked him up early. One Sunday we drove
to a military academy, boarding school
a possibility. The next year, we moved
to California, scent of orange
blossoms and salt air from the Pacific,
the clay fertile, you could be outside all day.
He thrived, ran varsity track, made the dean's list.
The army: four years in Iran, no leave, wolves
at the door in winter. Roses he planted in summer,
eaten by camels.   He thrived.

IV.

NARROW MARGINS

Patterns

In the dance pavilion wet with rain,
a memory of melon and berries.

Do you know this poet,
one who makes meatloaf
with brandy and Coke?

Now watching for any sign,
the drift season, October's slow
silvery veins.

On the back porch, winter boots stand ready,
mufflers smelling of mothballs
hang on wood pegs.

Aspens drop all their leaves in one day.
Bank the fires!
Dry winds from the Oregon border
thrash, split stalks horizontal.

Migrating tundra swans stream
through the Pacific Flyway.
Some say the ashen sky is common
this time of year.

Smoke changes things.
The old are dying.
Fear.
Uncertainty.

She says NO!
to worn-out clothes, rides the trolley downtown,
selects new fabric, herringbone
resembling geese
in formation
fleeing mechanical reaper blades.

Watching Autumn with Tu Fu

The lake still, most fishermen gone.
Small boats, one to each cabin sit dry docked.
Water moccasins, so threating
in summer, twine away
    to brimming waters.

On the country road, black walnuts
drop and split, the deep seam, an elk's eye.

Harvest moon, resplendent, anticipates
meandering spirits. Above the roar of traffic
on the interstate,
    shattering cricket screech,
wing rubbed raw, fiddlers out of tune.

I slip into a stupor, step onto the empty porch,
enjoy the creaking wood door,
    clapper tunes as it gently closes.

Beyond the dark beach, metal halide lamps
from a single fishing fleet
    burst vapor over blue.

Piñon

Mother warned: "Only bring home a solid head
of cabbage, lean pork chops, no soft potatoes."
Summer corn grew right down to the road, yet
I knew scant patterns of spring rains and new growth,

For the Washoe, Piñon harvest, the difference
between security and starvation, the nuts, a staple,
must be charred, ground down to flour.

My canister sits unopened, weevils set up house.
For my pesto, I select pine nuts from Trader Joe's,
so easy in a blender with basil and oil.

The Washoe leach wild spinach in a quick stream.
I rip the plastic bag, add moisture,
toss in the skillet with garlic and eggs.

I have a digital fork to test for doneness.
Women whittle a prized digging stick,
essential to probe for nutritious roots.

And in Autumn, a celebration, the *gumsaba*,
a well-fed population ready for ritual,
courtship and games.
            Carbon Footprints=Zero

I have no taboos during menses, do not have
to avoid cooking pots or jars of cured pickles.
Yet, hiking east of Carson City, I dare not
stumble and break the piñon's brittle limbs.

People in the Sun

Along Highway #99, a business off-site,
probably near Salida or Dinuba,
this motel selected for its cheap rates.

After A.M. meetings and a generic lunch
of tomato aspic, chicken and spice cake,
they enjoy a short break on a small patio.

Eyes closed, reclining in Adirondack chairs,
they could be on the deck of a cruise ship;
but these are not resort togs,
no salt air, just the acrid breeze
from pesticide factories.
The only vista, scrub grass
and purple wrinkles on low foothills.

I recognize this small group: civic workers
clothed in suits, ties, drab browns and grays,
gabardine or polyester, serviceable we say,
made to last until retirement.

One has a red tie,
hunches forward, studies notes.
Maybe the afternoon's keynote speaker?

Depleted by choices made, they return
to the boardroom glaring with artificial light.

Prufrock Eats a Donut

Mundane thoughts. Distracted
from revisions and accounts owed,
I wonder how many times I've written
about V shapes in the crotch of a tree?

Autumn. Nasty sand fleas
seem to have grown an extra set of teeth.
I stride out determined to search for
            spoke-like images.

I arrive at Spud-Nuts
(yes made with potatoes).
For inspiration, I analyze white space in donut holes.
Over cinnamon twists, two high school students
discuss Sartre.
        Am I hearing right?

Inspired, I drop off a packet of submissions
at the post office.

"Anything liquid, dangerous or toxic,"
the clerk asks?

        "No, only poetry."

Laughing, he begins to recite,

        "Let us go then you and I."

Customers stop shuffling,
            everyone listening.

Spring Equinox

Unpredictable temperatures.
Just as I put away the woolens,
a cold snap.
A farmer knows what to do:
look to fences, survey
winter's damage, calculate repairs,
turn the sheep out to graze.
The morning paper reports:
bitterns emerge from the reeds,
sturgeons glint mid-stream.
On the corner, the aging hippies
install a pink plastic flamingo,
but also quilt the bank
with tangerine lilies that outshine
the white cannas making the day
more than equal, more riotous.
Only half done what I meant to do,
setting aside volumes of New Age,
ethnographies, multiples on meditation.
I read the early poets
(what a friend calls fossils),
and pray with Robert Frost,
not to worry about what may or may not
be gathered in an *uncertain harvest.*
Just keep me here to ponder
all this sorting and fussing, these rituals
having nothing to do with clocks.

Watching Hummingbirds with Sun Tzu

Even in drought years they return to each bower
seeking milkweed, bog sage and brilliant cone flower,

then hover, blurred velocity dispersing mist,
mechanical whirligigs rearranging winter's dust.

A furious twirling, Chopin's *Minute Waltz* playing,
wings shears warping blue air, sweet roses fraying.

And in breeding season, boundaries soon plucked,
fiery gorgets alert, eyes penetrating a sullen roost.

One completes a pendulum swing, squeaking voice grating,
chick chick, chick chick, such a boisterous mating.

Another flies backward, sketching an aerial eclipse,
a grand reconnaissance, a shrilling, *vrrp vrrp, vrrp vrrp...*

Watching with Sun Tzu, we agree these diminutive wardens
know a good thing; all covet that same primordial garden.

Mid-afternoon. In a glass jar, remnants of fragrant Sun Tea.
I wonder about thresholds, the original Eden, the elusive sea.

Wild Doll

Easy to see she was well fed.
I want to reach in and touch the full cheeks.
Probably a tomboy with those cut bangs
and raised eyebrows.
Easy to see from the expensive dress,
probably found in an estate sale,
a collectible perhaps. Surprising, as Cornell
liked to go cheap: five and dime stores,
thrift shops and quirky finds in refuse cans.

Not your ordinary Tiny Tears
or perky Chatty Cathy,
more French porcelain and bisque,
more toddler than baby.
Not held much, not cuddled, not coddled.
Not tossed by mice and wind
to suffer dismemberment—
she survived intact,
plaid taffeta still bright.

These legs seem right for running,
a brief escape through summer fields.
From the road she sees him,
the quiet, outdoor type.

Playmate come out and play with me.

But all he does is fend off crows
and stand silent on his stick.
In the scent of molding hay, she reverses
steps, grabs the trellis to her room.
Too energetic, this one.

See her enshrined behind glass,
hiding behind a wicker fence,
field flowers in her hair?

Autumn Nocturne

A red tail hawk rests
in the heritage oak,
looks down on the ancients,
their fire, their chant, their verse.
You focus on drying milkweed,
the disappointed dragonfly,
crumbling bird house,
then dream of candlelight,
silk, a green meadow
and wake to river birch
scattering yellow butter pats.
Scenarios begin: that film
where the old house burns,
a distraught phone call,
the shrill siren from Folsom Prison.

little flower

A garden wedding
beyond the brick
walk, under the
rose arch covered
with a climbing
Joseph's Coat,
a halo of orange,
yellow, red. The
net skirt scratches,
patent leather shoes
pinch. Then
a reminder, pale
Cosmos brush
against her leg.
Steps slow
she moves soft
as satin, knows
there are blessings
in this basket.

Poet on a Mountain Top

A long trek to the splintered edge.
    Green foam boils off shore, vast distance
to other continents

yet he locates the vanishing point,
what converges, the first line and the last.

Retreating from the precipice, his walking stick
angles with the mountain,
    sandals slapping
            on the old footbridge.

He pauses on a stone bench, considers
writing about trees, remembers
that young sapling,
    orange phoenix perched on a tender limb.
With clear eyes, he even scribbled words
by galactic light.
    Now in opaque sun,
gnarled trunk, lichen splotched,
low branches clog with debris.

    Our poet squints.
    This was his tree!

At ocean's edge, generous stands
of new pines, spring green and dew wet,
    hook fast to boulders.

Today, not the last poem, but another, today.
Back bent, walking stick straight,
he moves down the path swept clean.

In My Dream, A Little Boat

I wait on the half-moon bridge.
Ahead bold flowers glisten

and plentiful birds with open
wings gaily sing. The way I

came is steep and filled with
too many broken chairs to return

even if I remove my shoes and
walk backwards. I cannot decide.

Snows have come and gone.
More will be required of me.

Unable to go forward,
I cannot compete with trees.

My brush paints a ladder
of purple silk. As I descend

a little boat comes for me
over the deep and wrinkled stream.

Centuries
Homegrown angel who I had met before and had largely since forgotten
~Charles Simic

1. 1950

The version from my grandfather.
Before he was born, his older brother, still little, so excited
to see the train coming, tracks below the grand home (a Federalist style),
couldn't stop, ran right into the train.
I didn't know his name, he wasn't listed
in family records.

2. 2000-2014

I've returned so many times: walking the rails.
taking photos, caught up in the sharpness of Seagram's Distillery,
lush green fields where Ohio, Indiana and Kentucky meet,
Shawnee burial mounds next to the family cemetery,
Revolutionary War remains along with their wives and children,
one-room school house now a private residence, church now
a real estate office: Twain country: tobacco,
living horses and paddle boats,

I forgot to remember him.

3. April 25, 2017

A cousin forwards an email from a diligent librarian,
barely legible in old script dated, April 25, 1882.

Cincinnati Daily Gazette
Special Dispatch

Killed by the Locomotive
**As the train on the Big Five Road approached Lawrenceburg
Junction, Hydman Stevens, three-year-old son of Charles
a local farmer of that neighborhood, was seen sitting on
a cross-tie. The engineer reported he tried to reverse.
Medical assistance was requested by telegraph, Dr. Gatch
summoned, but too late. A playmate managed to get off
the tracks in time.**

June, 2017

I can imagine a small boy sliding down
the cherry wood bannister, watching
from the porch: billowing steam, iron horse huffing.

Then after, every day, mother and father
listening for the creaking cars,
my grandfather taking the same train back and forth
twenty miles to college.

It is said, eternity lasts a day, a year, as long
as someone remembers us. After 137 years, astronomical!
What can I do to keep a life sacred?
(Mircea Eliade suggests, the only true reality is in ritual.)

I don't know if I will return from the west,
but if I do—can I at least place a small wagon,
a toy bear near the cross-tie under the protective paw-paw?

His name was Hydman.

Glass

Four-year old Cassandra
survived brain cancer,
surgery and radiation.
She is aware
that other children may not
speak but stare at her baldness
and twin scars. To her,
their eyes make a click sound—
open/shut
like a doll's stiff lashes.
Through the window, *she sees*
a boy alone...shooting baskets.
He sees dark eyes and waves.
Her hands raise
to the cool glass. Outside,
he kneels, places his on hers,
palm to palm. All four
move in unison,
like the Ouija board's
heart-shaped planchette
searches and finds answers
in a lighter touch. The sun shines
on the boy with bright eyes.
A long time
since the mother
has heard such laughter.
She watches
in silence, letting joy happen.

In this Room Everyone Behaved

I'm at the front door, remembering
the light panel, the pane that cut my hand.
A boy struck my sister with a piece of coal;
I was frantically knocking for help.
Inside the living room, I'm looking at the baby grand
where mother and grandfather played tunes by ear:
"Little Brown Jug" and "Hawaiian Love Call."
I see the bench filled with advanced sheet music,
Czerny and Bach, and my own beginner's
John Thompson with a few faded stickers
on barely learned pieces, and in front of the fireplace,
andirons with carved bear profiles. In the corner
sat the Philco with its green eye.
Look, I'm there with my brother on Saturday morning
listening to "Let's Pretend," or writing down
instructions for the number of box tops
needed for a Wonder Woman ring.
Here is the stack of Life Magazines
that came every Friday and reported every war.
This room was a place where we all behaved,
where the insurance man sat on the sofa to renew policies.
Near the front window, the Christmas tree glittered
in a swath of angel hair and Noma lights.
This is where we acted up when the sitter
(old Mrs. Selby) came; we did cartwheels,
tossed popcorn, and were sent to bed.
The night my Dad worked swing shift,
a young sitter had a party, the room filled with sailors.
Next morning Schlitz beer cans dotted the lawn,
and neighbors clucked their tongues.
The drapes with cabbage roses are missing,
the designer wall paper gone.
A family fist fight required a call to the cops.
I recall the aroma of pork chops, the soft clink of china
as mother hand-washed the dishes.
See us in front of the radio for the news
or a comedy? Dad rests in his chair, smokes
a Lucky Strike and reads *The Indianapolis Star*.
In this room—we all behaved.

American Bittern

A dark eye swivels.
If I had looked away
just before, I would have missed
speckled wedges, chips
like a Klimt painting: bronze,
ochre and lime green spliced
among cattails. My eye
struggles to keep up
with this fleeting image
like imprinting a memory:
attention-selection-retrieval.
Just a hint, a piece to build
that fear again, dark alleyway,
pebbles rattling deep cracks
in the center, an overused
worry stone. Or the eye chart,
click of the lens: blur, fuzz,
which memory
is correct, A or B?
Which is better, B or A?
When I leave that thought,
the bittern suddenly thrusts
a slow beak to the sky,
becomes a vertical shaft,
one with the reeds, invisible.
The riverbank now quiet,
November grasses in still water
barely move. Colors dissolve
my blinker's moment.

A Narrow Margin of Color

White star scented air, dry and crisp
at 6,000 feet. The moon with a large ring,
translucent, ocular fuzz.
We step out at midnight,
a monochromatic nocturne.
The sky tinged with a barely-there-blue
we admire soft light on snow,
Tamarack's black trunks
and thin shadows of wintering dogwood.
A glacial spectrum. I think moongarten,
and know night owns this landscape.

Next day, on snowshoes,
we trek the meadow, sun so bright,
a quick stop to rest our eyes.
There in deep shade,
a neon blue that disappears in bright sun.
You say, "It's the water content
that makes the crystals seem electrified,
filament lit from within."
We stomp around trees, in and out
of light, testing our perception.

I've seen the sign above small taverns,
a martini glass with an olive just-that-blue,
and on paint chips: *Feather Falls,*
Peace River, June Lake, Carthage...
but the closest I come—Chagall's pencil,
writing the sky over Vitebsk.

Notes

Part I.
"Ruins are Never Empty." Title, a line after John O'Donohue.
  Anam Cara.
"At the Community Garden." Inspired by *Locke, 1928* a novel
  by Shawna Yang Ryan. It was renamed *Water Ghosts.*
  "Women appear out of the river and disrupt the town."

Part II.
"Extinguished Stars." A few lines by Wislawa Szymborska
  and Omar Khayyan.
"Rocket Man." Poem cited: "First Cave," Jane Segler.
"Winter Coat Tinged Platinum." Inspired by Tony Kendrew.

Part III.
"Composition IX." Painting by Vasily Kandinsky.
"Bloodstone." Inspired by *You flare into a room like a sunburst.*
  Ghalib.
"Against Insomnia. A translitic. "Insomnia." Dana Gioia,
translated by Gustavo Solórzano-Alfaro
"Where Beelines End." Source: "Lindenbloom," Amy Clampett.
  "Virgil's Bees," Carol Ann Duffy. "Falling Asleep in the Garden,"
  David Waggoner.
"*Gelée blanche.*" A Painting by Camille Pissarro. Note: "Pissarro
  commits the grave error of painting fields with shadows cast
  by trees placed outside the frame. The viewer is left to suppose
  they exist." Critic, Jules Antoine Castagnary, *LeSiècle,* 29
  April 1874.
"Her Name is Yolen." Photo, Ariana Cubillos, AP Images.
  National Geographic, September 2008.

Part IV.
"Piñon." Source: *The Two Worlds of the Washoe: An Indian
  Tribe of California and Nevada.* Janes F. Downs.
  Stanford University, 1966.
"People in the Sun." Painting by Edward Hopper.
"Spring Equinox." Cited: "A Prayer in Spring." Robert Frost.
"Wild Doll." *Bébé Marie* by Joseph Cornell
"Poet on a Mountain Top." Ink and color handscroll,
  Shen Chow.

Jeanine Stevens is a California poet by way of Indiana. Books include: *No Lunch Among the Day Stars,* Cold River Press, *Limberlost* and *Inheritor,* Future Cycle Press and *Sailing on Milkweed,* Cherry Grove Collections. She has a number of chapbooks including award winning *Gertrude Sitting: Portraits of Women,* Heartland Review Chapbook Contest, and *Brief Immensity,* Finishing Line Press Prize in Poetry. Other awards are from The McGuffin Poet Hunt, William Stafford Award, The Ekphrasis Prize, The Stockton Arts Commission, WOMR Cape Cod Community Radio National Poetry Contest, Western Archipelago Review, Mendocino Coast Writer's Conference, and Soulmaking. Jeanine's poetry has appeared in *Evansville Review, North Dakota Quarterly, Chiron Review, So it Goes: Journal of the Kurt Vonnegut Memorial Library, Rosebud* and *Muse.* She has been editor of newsletters, judged poetry contests and served as poetry workshop facilitator. She studied poetry at U.C. Davis and CSU Sacramento, has an M.A. in Anthropology and a doctorate in Education. Jeanine is Professor Emerita at American River College and a member of the Community of Writers. She lives in Sacramento and Lake Tahoe with her husband Greg Chalpin.

www.ingramcontent.com/pod-product-compliance
Lightning Source LLC
Chambersburg PA
CBHW011231120626
46549CB00008B/3226